This is a story about Officer Frank.  He is a Police Officer.  He is our friend, and his job is to help us and protect us.

While Officer Frank is at work he wears special clothes called a uniform. He also wears a special belt that carries all of his equipment.

Let's look at his uniform and all of his equipment!

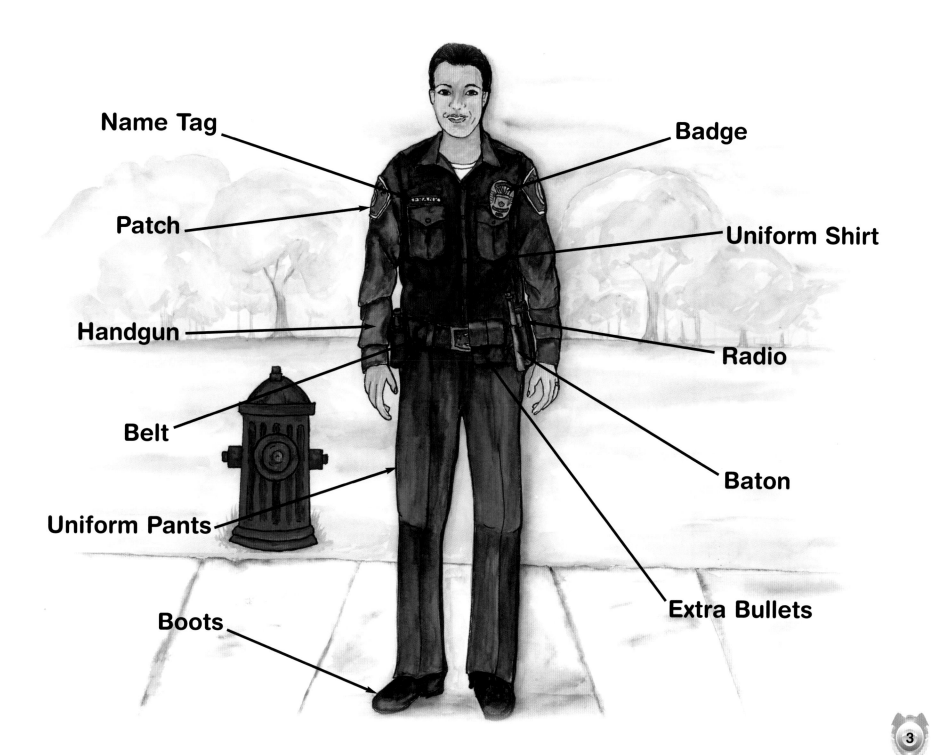

Name Tag

Badge

Patch

Uniform Shirt

Handgun

Radio

Belt

Baton

Uniform Pants

Boots

Extra Bullets

3

While Officer Frank is at work, he drives a police car. Look! Officer Frank is waving to us. Let's say "Hi" and wave back to him.

This is Officer Frank's police car. It is black and white on the outside and has blue and red lights on top. Let's look inside his police car and see all of the equipment he uses while he is at work.

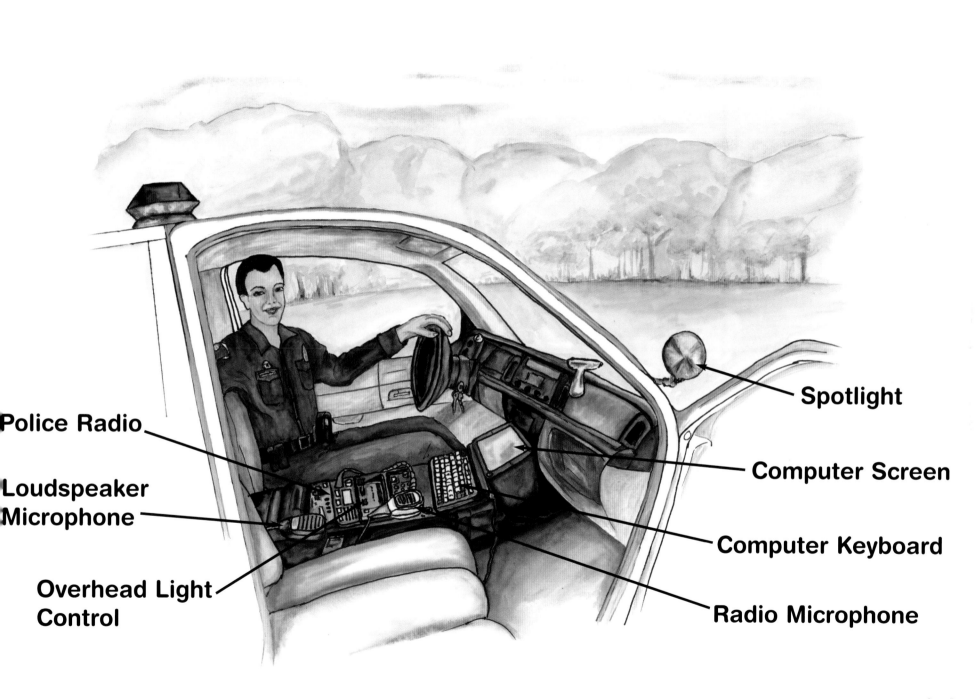

**Spotlight**

**Police Radio**

**Loudspeaker Microphone**

**Overhead Light Control**

**Computer Screen**

**Computer Keyboard**

**Radio Microphone**

Officer Frank drives his police car near your school to make sure you and your friends are safe while you learn and play.

Sometimes Officer Frank visits your classroom to teach you about how to live a safe life. He also likes to play games with you during recess. Wow! Look at him kick the ball high in the air!

While you are sleeping, he drives down your street and protects your neighborhood.

Officer Frank even works on special days, like Halloween, so you will be safe while you trick-or-treat.

It is very important to Officer Frank that you and your family have a safe holiday season. That's why he patrols your neighborhood during this special time.

Sometimes he works while you are eating dinner with your family.

When Officer Frank is not working he likes to do things just like you. Look, he is playing basketball with his friends. What color shirt is Officer Frank wearing?

While he is at home he likes to watch T.V.

He also enjoys reading books.

Officer Frank likes many of the same foods that you do. Sometimes he likes to go out for pizza with his friends.

Officer Frank also enjoys spending time with his family, just like you do.

You see, Officer Frank is just like you and me!